HAROLD CROMWELL

Pen Drawings
of
Back in the old
DAYS

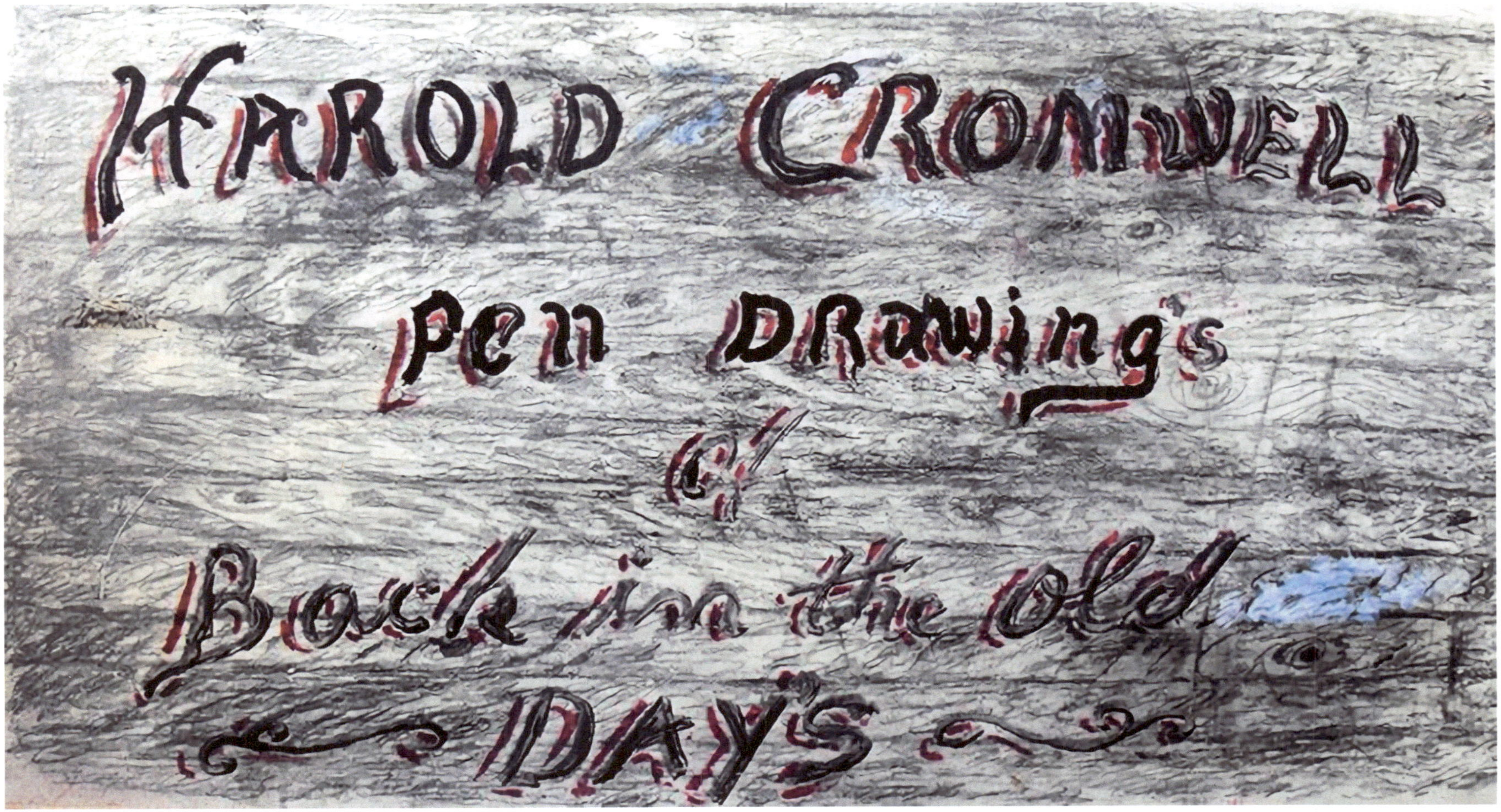

Back in the Old Days: The Art of Harold Cromwell
© 2023 ARCAC

All images: Harold Cromwell
Cover design: Rebekah Wetmore
Editor: Andrew Wetmore

ISBN: 978-1-998149-22-3
First edition September, 2023

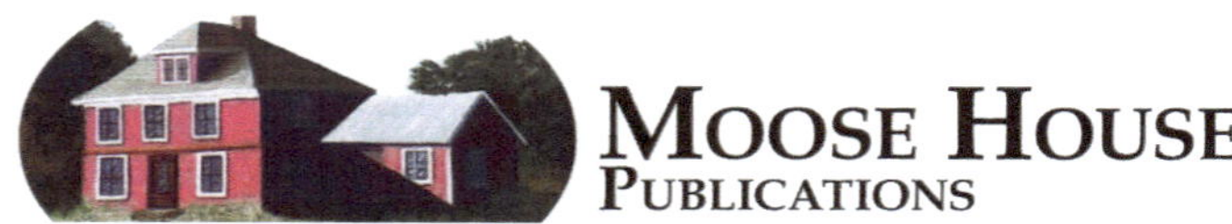

MOOSE HOUSE
PUBLICATIONS

2475 Perotte Road
Annapolis County, NS
B0S 1A0

moosehousepress.com
info@moosehousepress.com

We live and work in Mi'kma'ki, the ancestral and unceded territory of the Mi'kmaw People. This territory is covered by the "Treaties of Peace and Friendship" which Mi'kmaw and Wolastoqiyik (Maliseet) People first signed with the British Crown in 1725. The treaties did not deal with surrender of lands and resources but in fact recognized Mi'kmaq and Wolastoqiyik (Maliseet) title and established the rules for what was to be an ongoing rela‑ tionship between nations. We are all Treaty people.

The Art of Harold Cromwell

This exhibition of work by Harold Cromwell at ARTSPLACE, the home of the Annapolis Region Community Arts Council, reintroduces the art world to a folk artist who has been somewhat eclipsed by his more famous peers, such as his near contemporary (and near neighbour), Maud Lewis, one of the few Canadian artists to become a household name.

But Harold Cromwell, despite not receiving the sustained attention enjoyed by Lewis (and to a lesser extent by other artists who have received national and international attention from galleries and collectors, such as Joe Norris, Collins Eisenhauer, Ralph Boutilier, Joe Sleep, and Sidney Howard), is considered by professionals in the art world as one of the most important folk artists in the country. That recognition, however, has taken a longer time coming than the obvious quality of his work would suggest.

Cromwell has a unique style and approach that sets him apart from other first wave folk artists, and it is only a matter of time before his reputation grows outside of professional circles.

Maud Lewis rose to prominence in the 1960s, and the other Nova Scotia folk artists in her peer group were first brought to national attention with the 1976 touring exhibition Folk Art of Nova Scotia, organized by the Art Gallery of Nova Scotia and curated by Bernard Riordon. From that point on, Nova Scotia Folk Art became a major part of Nova Scotia's visual art legacy, with numerous group and solo exhibitions that have kept the genre in the forefront of the public eye.

Harold Cromwell wasn't included in that first exhibition, or in other early touring shows of Nova Scotia Folk Art, but by the 1990s his work was regularly included in any survey of the genre, and has been on view regularly at the Art Gallery of Nova Scotia for three decades.

There is no formula, of course, for why one artist achieves fame and another, seemingly of equal talent, does not. Hard work plays a role, of course, but art is always hard work—no work, no art. There is a combination of factors that cannot be predicted. Luck, basically.

Nor does fame always bring personal success or satisfaction: Maud Lewis, of course, lived in poverty and had been deceased for decades before becoming the household name that she is now. Whether fame is the result of luck or fate, its effects are often only visible afterwards.

But perhaps fame is about to catch up with Harold Cromwell.

Though he hasn't been accorded the same level of recognition as Lewis and others, Weymouth's Harold Cromwell is certainly one of the giants of Nova Scotia folk art. Cromwell had deep roots in Southwest Nova Scotia. He was born in Weymouth Falls in 1919 and was descended from Black Loyalists who settled in the area in 1783. Many of the Black Loyalists had been slaves in the United States and had earned both freedom and land grants by serving in the British Army.

Cromwell, too, served, as a soldier in the Canadian army during the Second World War (included in this exhibition is a drawing harking back to his time in the army).

Unlike Lewis, Norris or Eisenhauer, Cromwell was neither a painter nor a carver, working primarily with the humble materials of pencil and ball-point pen on plain white paper or wood. For over 50 years Cromwell, though his drawings, depicted memories, stories and anecdotes of daily life, especially in the African Nova Scotian community of Weymouth Falls and area. Occasionally he used colour, both in paintings and drawings (and there are examples in this exhibition), but, as one of his handmade signs attests, it was the pen that was his primary artistic tool, and nostalgia that was his primary theme: "pen drawings of back in the old days," his sign reads.

Harold Cromwell sold his work at the Annapolis Royal Farmers' & Traders' Market, and for many years he was artist-in-residence at Upper Clements Park. He was extremely prolific, but his work was never the subject of a major exhibition (though it was the subject of a festival at Sissiboo Landing in Weymouth in 2017). David Woods, then-curator of African Nova Scotia Art at the AGNS, said upon Cromwell's death in 2008, "He would have been a Canadian folk art icon had the public seen the scope of his works."[1]

Unfortunately, the public has never had that chance. Until now, that is, with the exhibition Back in the Old Days: The Art of Harold Cromwell.

Cromwell was unique among the major Nova Scotia folk artists in two ways—he was African Nova Scotian (indeed, the most widely known African Nova Scotian folk artist in Canada), and his work consisted primarily of monochrome drawings (Joe Sleep also drew, but most of his work was done with coloured pens and inks).

He would draw on any scrap of paper that came to hand—even paper plates (Royal Chinet, of course, made here in Nova Scotia). There is one paper plate drawing in this exhibition, and another in the collection of the Canadian Museum of History. Obviously, he would draw on almost anything when the spirit moved him.

Folk art is so popular because it seems more accessible, lacking the perceived seriousness of so-called "high art." Like that of many of his peers, his art looked back to an idealized Nova Scotian past, one of close-knit community and family life. This vision may not have reflected what life was always like, but it certainly spoke to how Cromwell aspired for it to have been.

While Cromwell was in the military hospital at Debert, recuperating from wounds received overseas during the Second World War, he was given drawing materials by the nurses to help him pass the time. He soon started drawing the doctors and nurses, as well as the landscape he saw out the window. Drawing became a defining part of his life, much more than a simple pastime.

After the war he worked as a miner in Sudbury, Ontario. After five years he returned to Weymouth, where he worked several jobs, always drawing in his spare time. After his retirement he took up drawing more intensely.

---

1   David Woods, quoted by John DeMings on NovaNewsNow.com, posted March 31, 2008.

While the bulk of his work was monochromatic and modest in scale, in later years he also made larger works in which he used markers or coloured pencils to add splashes of colour to his drawings. He often included texts in his drawings—some purely descriptive and others humorous. He even made drawings and paintings on the walls of his home.

Cromwell's work depicts life in a rural community in the early twentieth century and is laced with humour and wry observation. While Cromwell's work is included in the collections of the Art Gallery of Nova Scotia and The Canadian Museum of History, much of his work is held in private collections, and to date institutions have struggled to secure the funding to mount exhibitions of this important artist's work.

With the opening of this exhibition of his work at ARTSPLACE, that long neglect is coming to an end. It is likely that, with this public exposure, renewed public and professional interest will propel Harold Cromwell's art further into the spotlight, as is only fitting for such a major figure in the history of Nova Scotian, and indeed, Canadian, folk art.

Ray Cronin
Elmsdale, Nova Scotia, 2023

Back in the Old Days: The Art of Harold Cromwell

Winteny's back in 1934-1942

Pen and ink – 12 3/8" x 19 5/8"

Bottom left:
Winteny's Barl Stove Mill Back in 1934-42 Weymouth

Bottom right:
Winteny's Mill in Weymouth in 1931-40 est

Back:

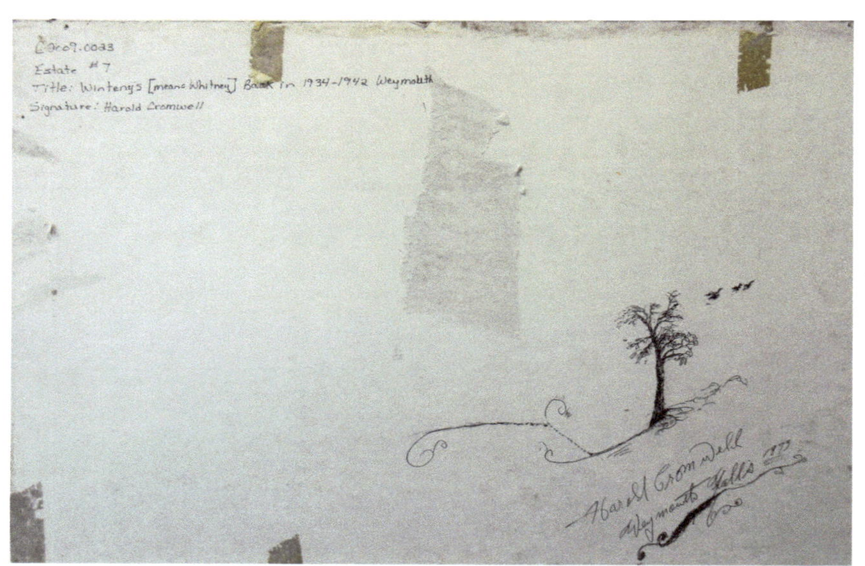

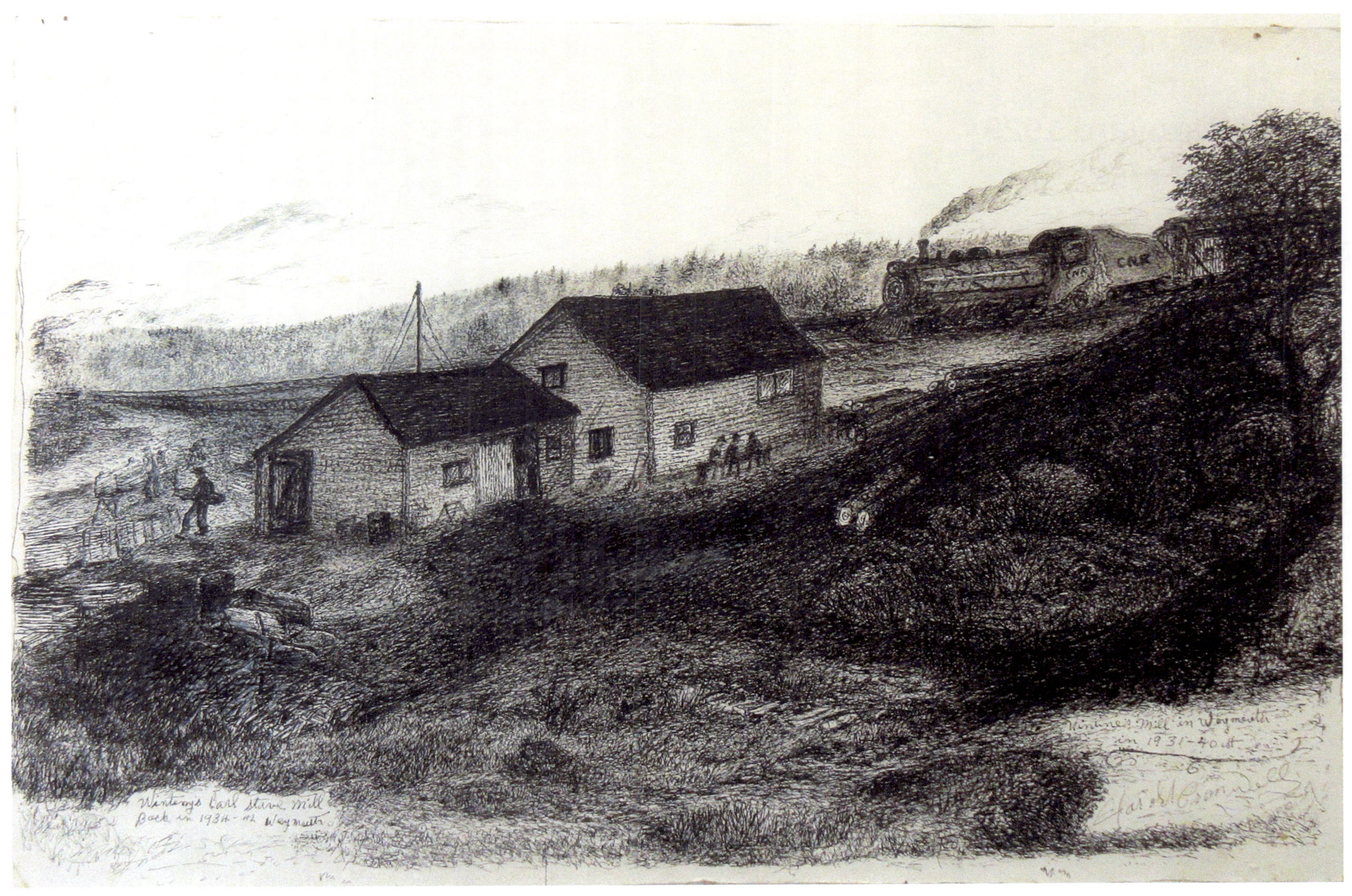
Winter's Barl stave Mill
Back in 1934 - 42 Weymouth
Winters Mill in Weymouth
in 1931 - 40 st
Harold Cromwell

The Old Barnyard 1929

Pen and ink – 9 3/8" x 11 ¾"

Bottom left:
The old Barn yard 1929

Bottom right:
Old Barn of 1929

Back:

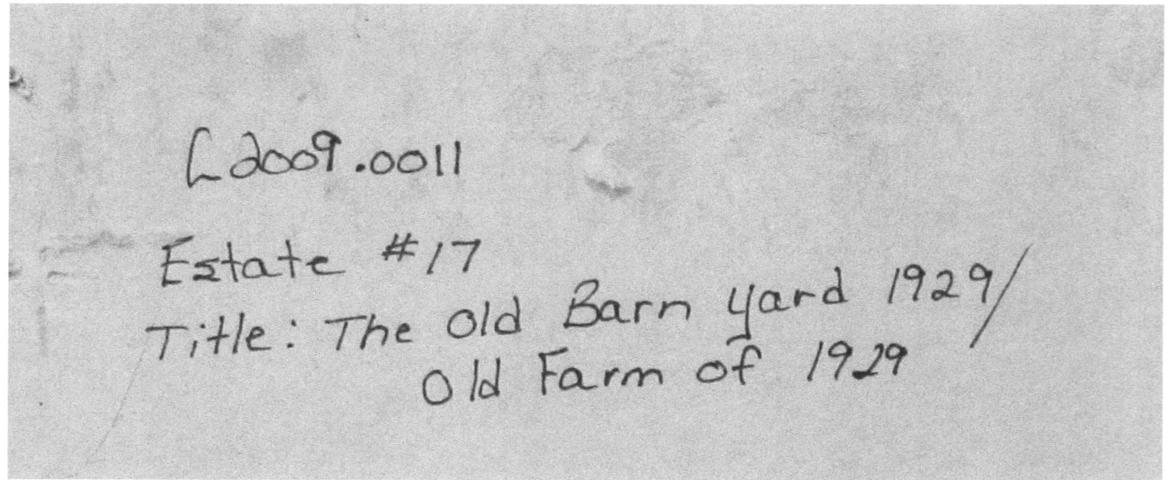

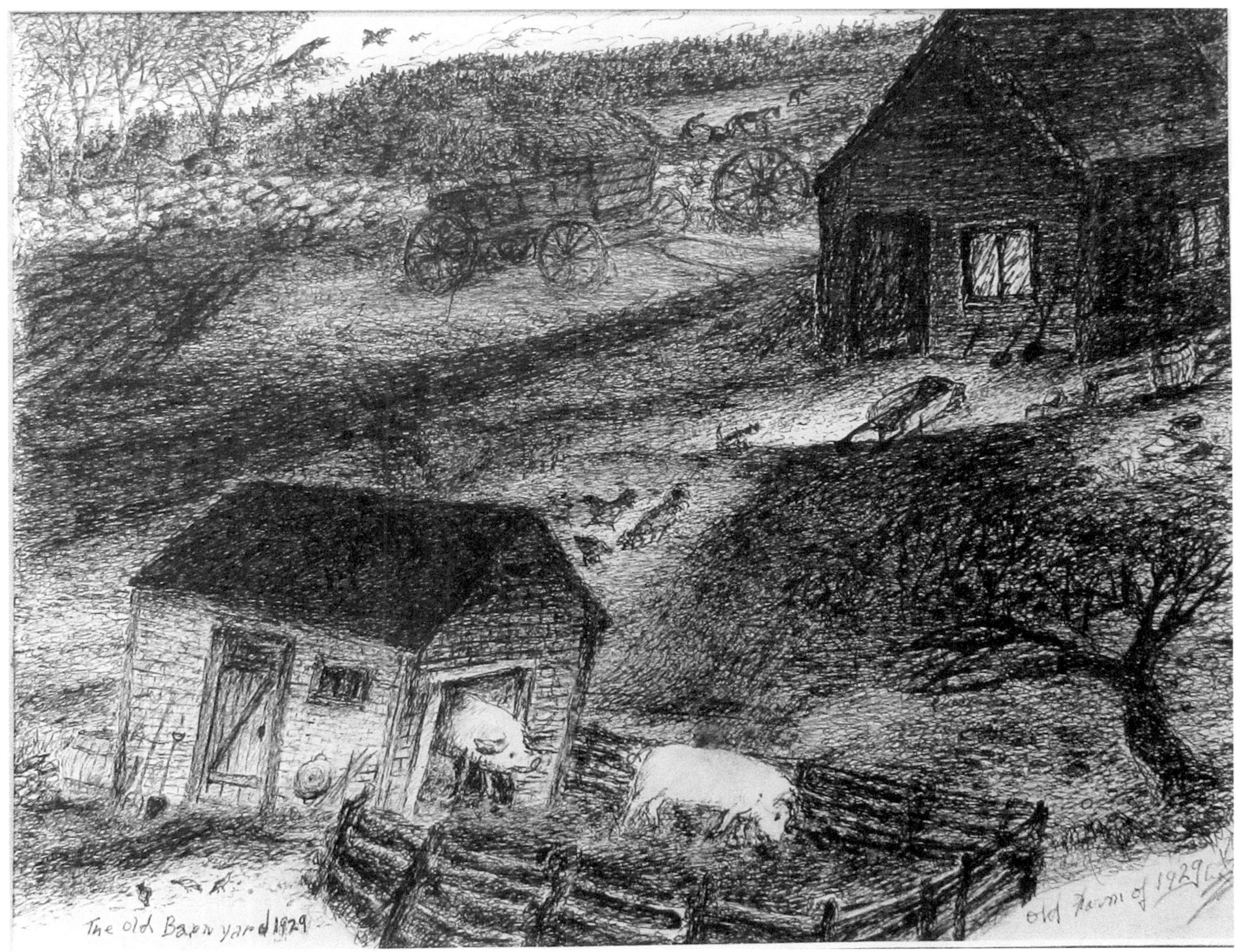
The old Barn yard 1929
old farm of 1929

Ser may we sleep in your Barn Tonigh?

Pen and ink – 10 ¼" x 12 ¾"

Bottom:
Ser may we sleep in your Barn Tonigh?
Yes you have to Pick two Barl's of Apples before you lay down

Back in 1938

Back:

L2009. 0031
Estate #11
Title: Ser (sic) May we sleep in your Barn tonigh (sic)?
Yes, you Have To Pick Two Barl's (sic) of Apple's Before you Lay Down
Signature: Harold Cromwell

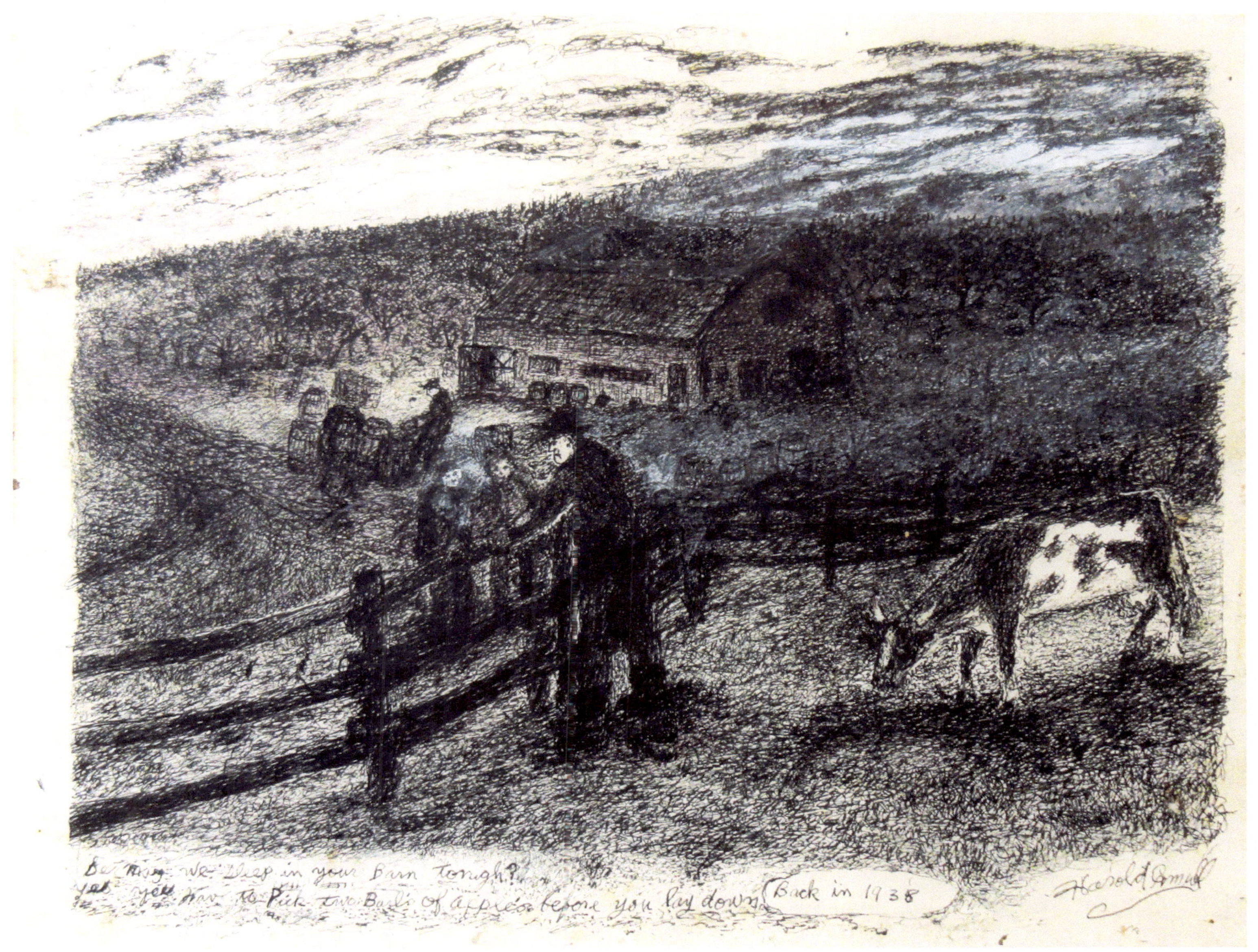
Be_ may we sleep in your barn tonigh?
yes. yes. you hav to Pick two Barls of apples before you lay down
Back in 1938
Harold Cromwell

Sam Langford School, Weymouth Falls

Pen and ink – 14 ¼" x 18 3/8"

Top left:
Sam Langford in Early age Boston Tar Body

Top centre:
Weymouth Falls School from 1878-1950

Top right:
Sam Langford At Weymouth Falls in – in 1920

On monument:
Sam Langford School Weymouth Falls

Back:

C2009.0071
Estate # 3
Title. Sam Langford School Weymouth Falls
Signature: Harold Cromwell

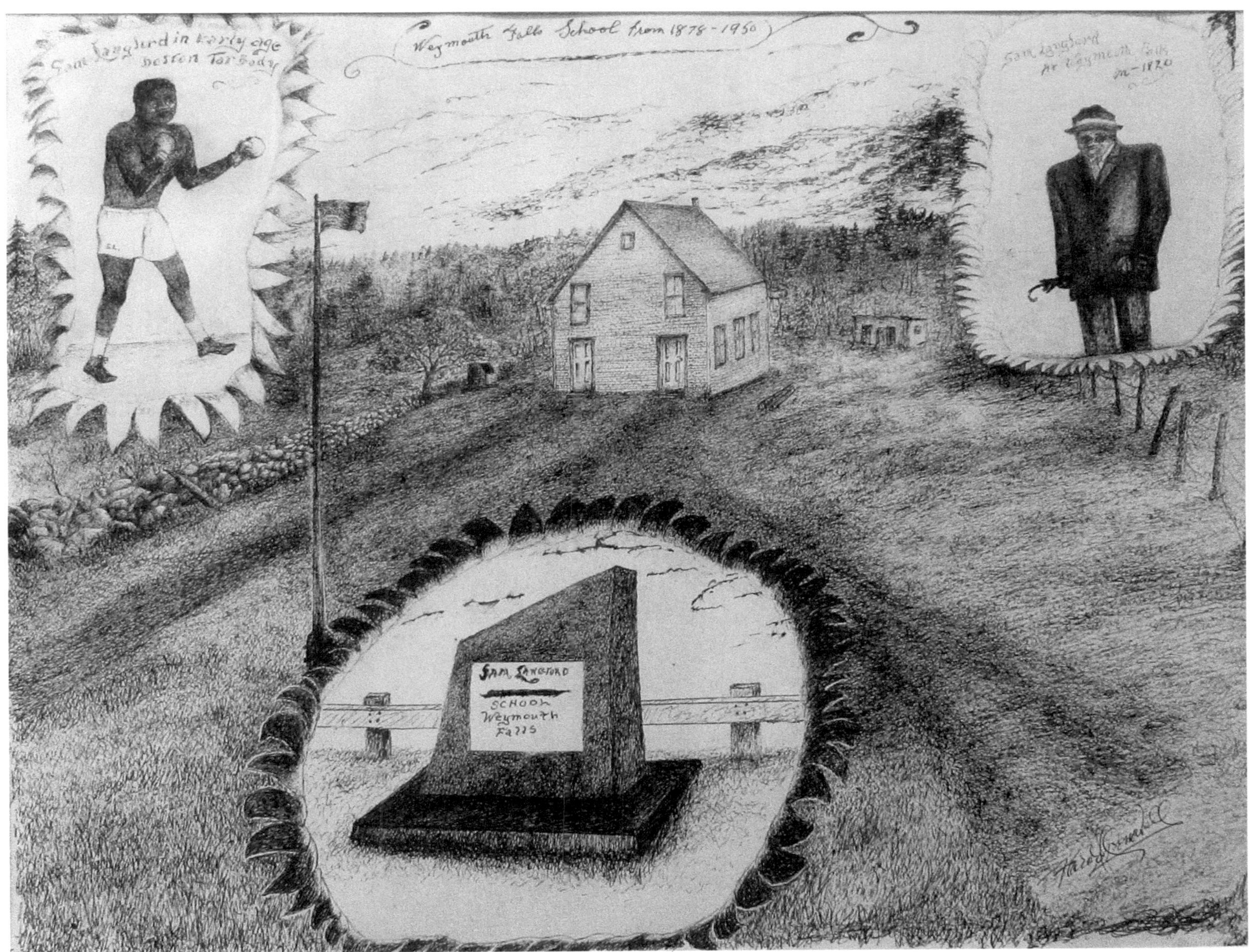
Sam Langford in early age Boston Tor body
Weymouth Falls School from 1878 - 1950
Sam Langford at Weymouth Falls in 1920
SAM LANGFORD
SCHOOL
Weymouth
Falls

Less We Forget

Pen and ink – 21 ½" x 27 ¾"

Top left:
XRAY
ARMY RECRUITS

Top centre:
BOBS PUB

Top right:
a Battle in Scotland 1942

Centre left:
Troops line up with mess tins

Centre:
Just a small hapening of England & Scotland 1941

Bottom:
LESS WE FORGET

Back:

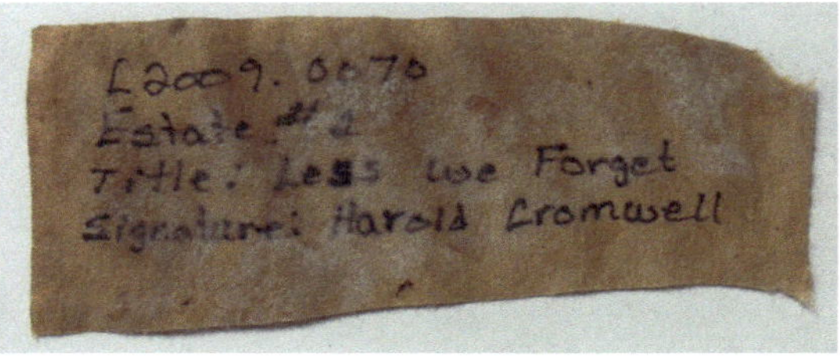

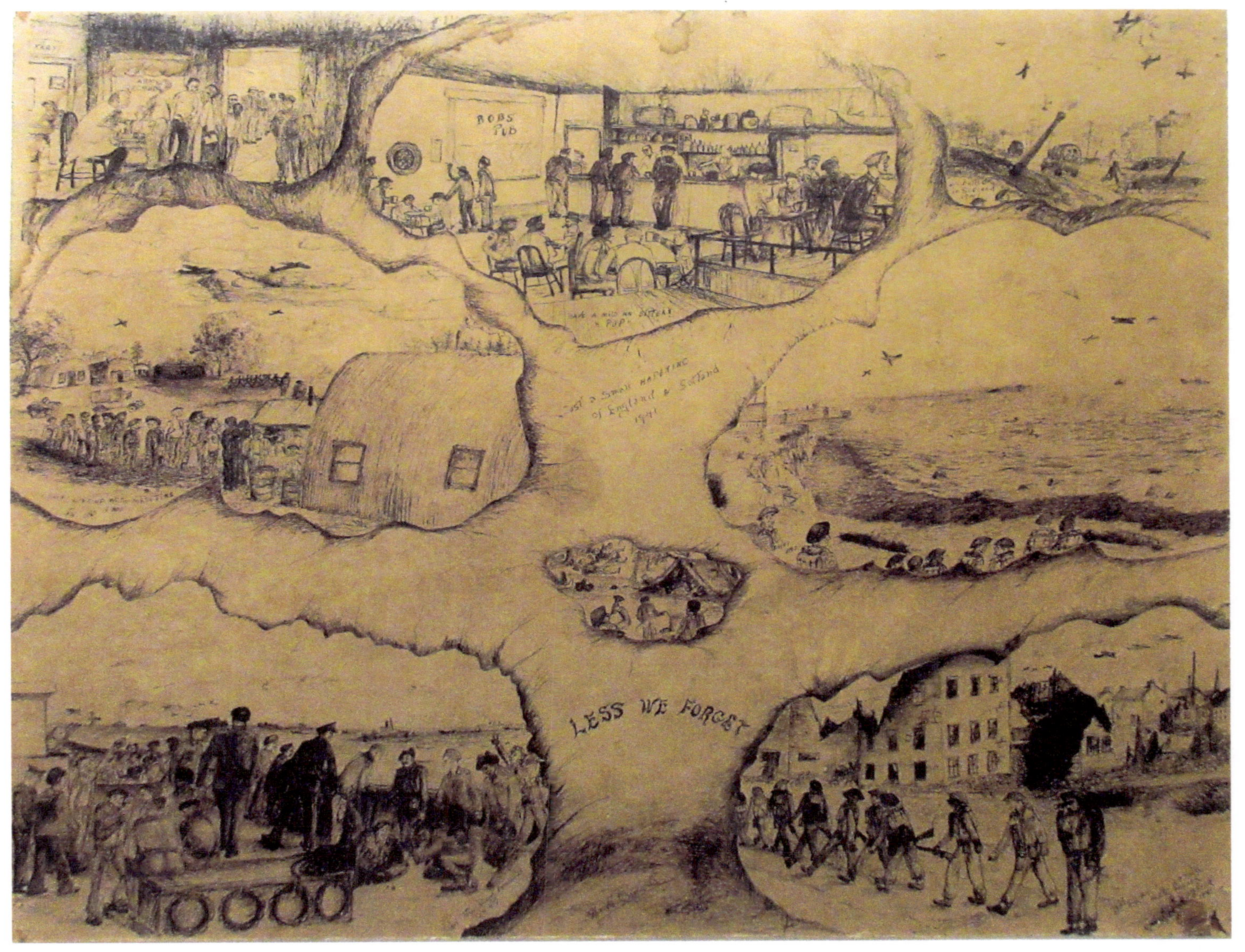
BOBS PUB
LESS WE FORGET

Old Run Down Camp

Pen, ink and coloured pencil – 8 3/8" x 11 1/8"

Bottom:
Old run down camp

Back:

C2009.0072
Estate #
Title: Old Run Down Camp
Signature: Harold Cromwell

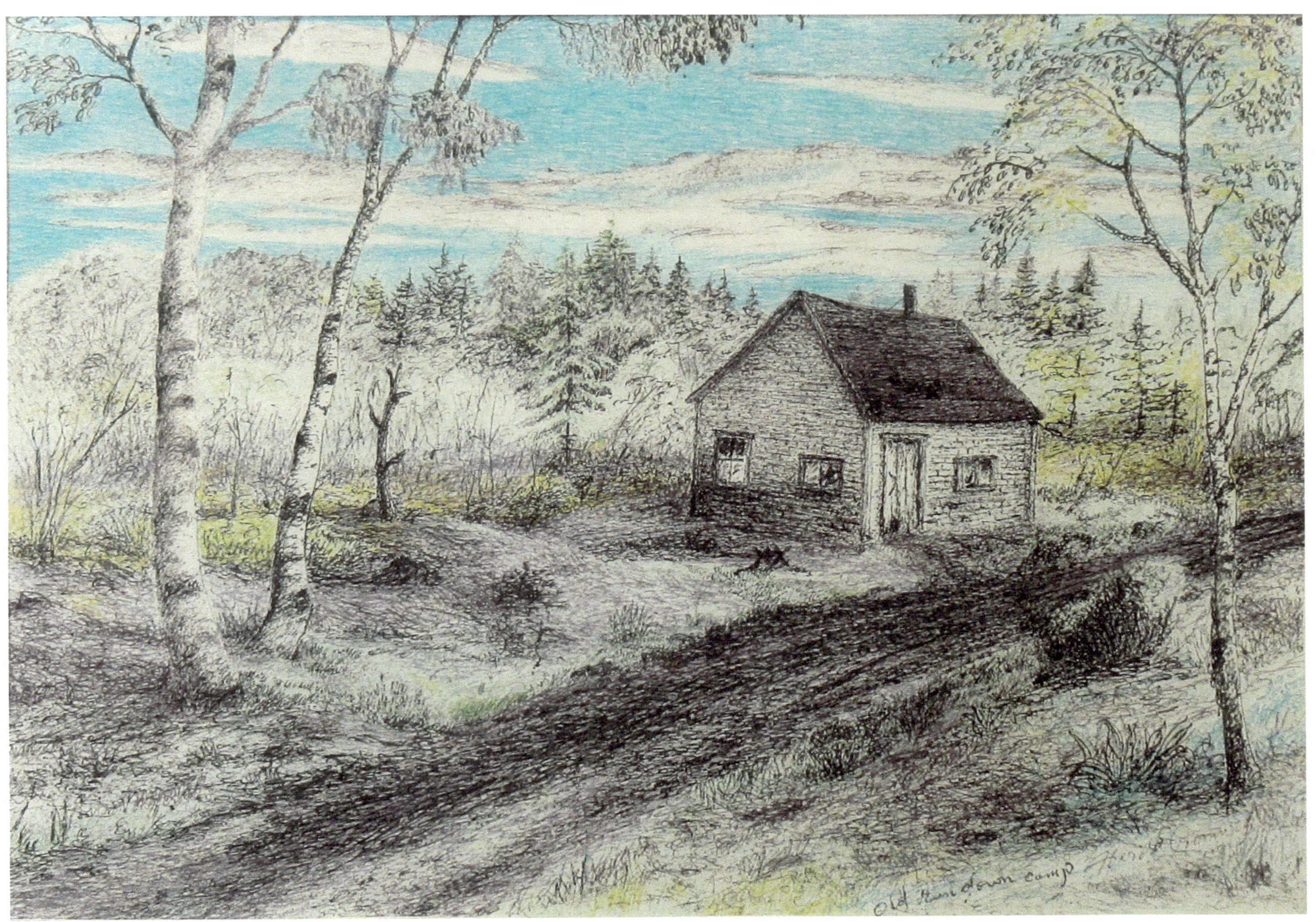
Old Rundown camp

Hunters Haveing a Card Game Be Were of the Big Cat CUGER

Pen and ink – 9 7/8" x 12 ¾"

Bottom left:

Hunters haveing a card game
be were of the big cat CUGER

Back:

L2009.0030
Estate # 15
Title: Hunters Haveing (sic) a Card Game
        Be Were (sic) of the Big Cat Luger (sic)
Signature: Harold Cromwell

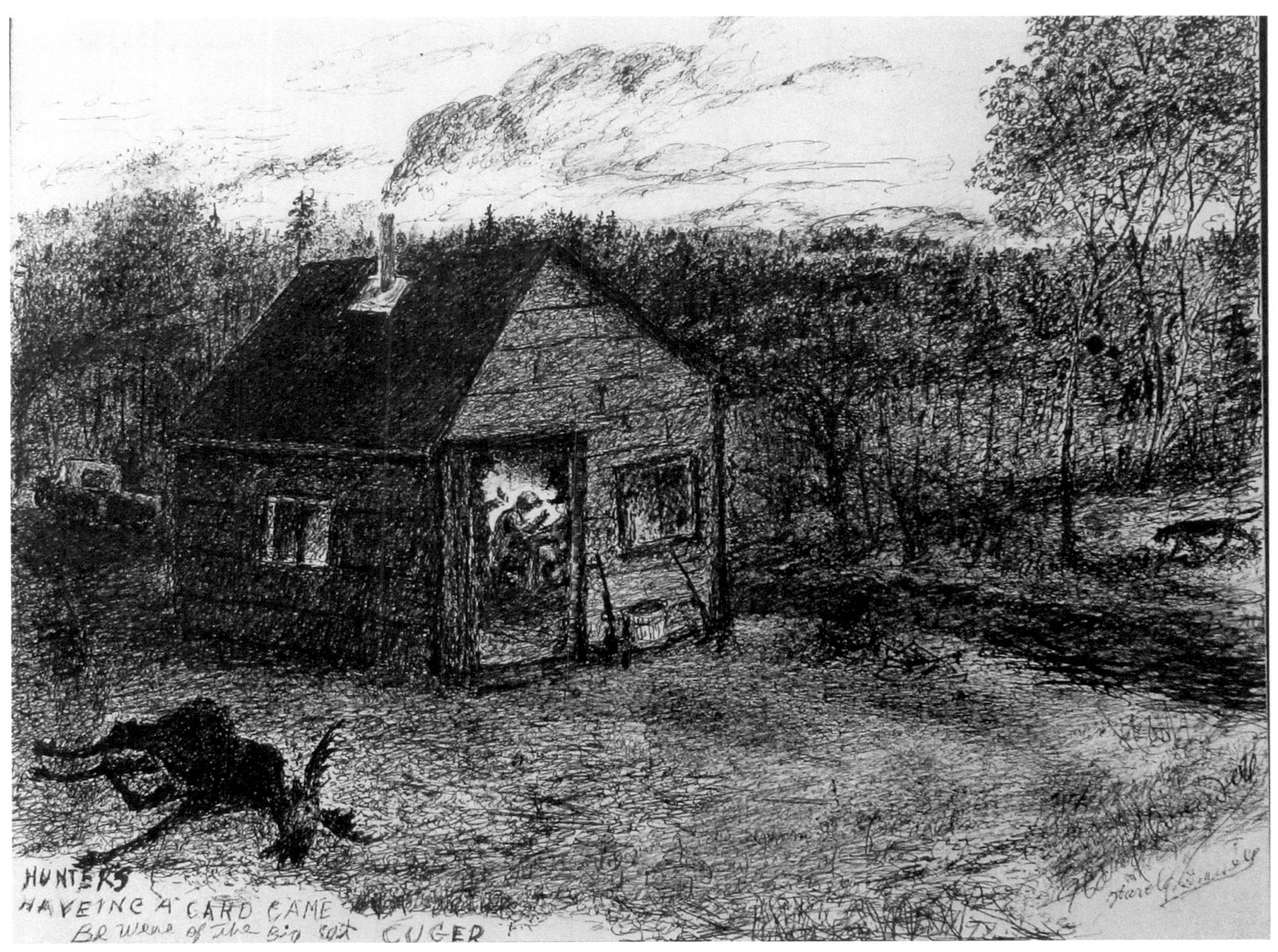
HUNTERS
HAVEING A CARD GAME
Be Ware of The Big Fox   CUGER

A Farmer's Market

Pen, ink and gouache – 12 ¼" x 17 5/8"

Bottom:
A Farmer's Market

Back:

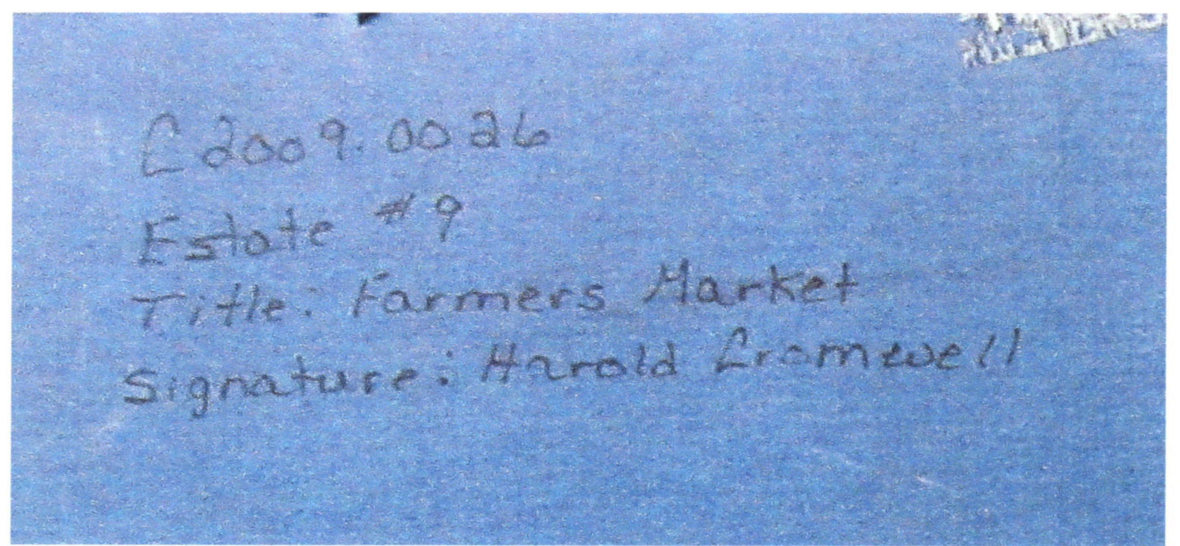

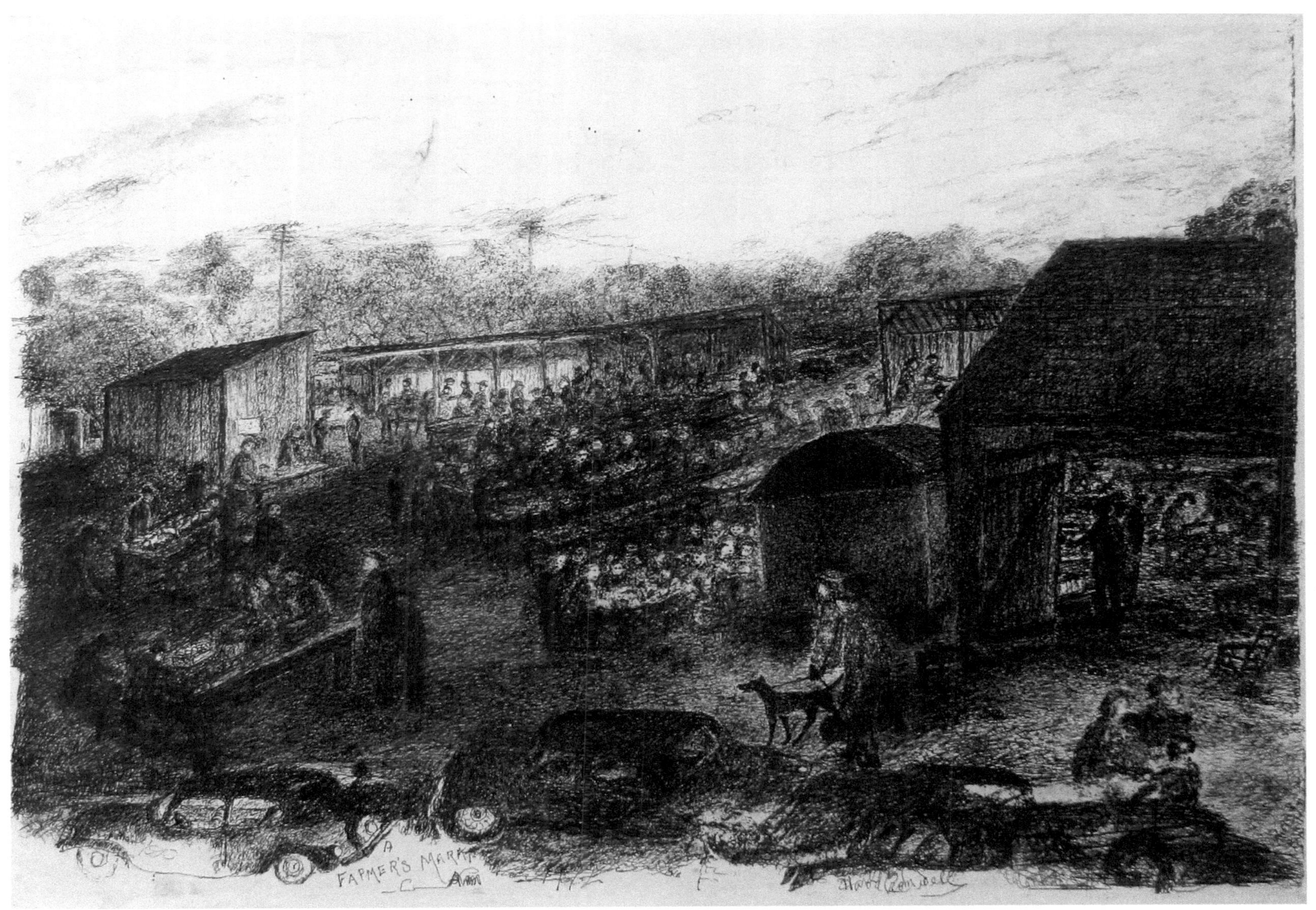
A FARMER'S MARKET
Harold Cromwell

Good Old Hunting Groungs and Camp, Back in the Good Old Days 1928

Pen, ink and watercolour - 9 ¾" x 12 ¾"

Bottom right:
good old Hunting groungs and Camp
Back in the good old Days
1928

Back:

C2009.0067
Estate #___ (not supplied)
Title: Good old Hunting Groungs (sic) and camp
       Back in the Good Old Days 1928

Signature: Harold Cromwell

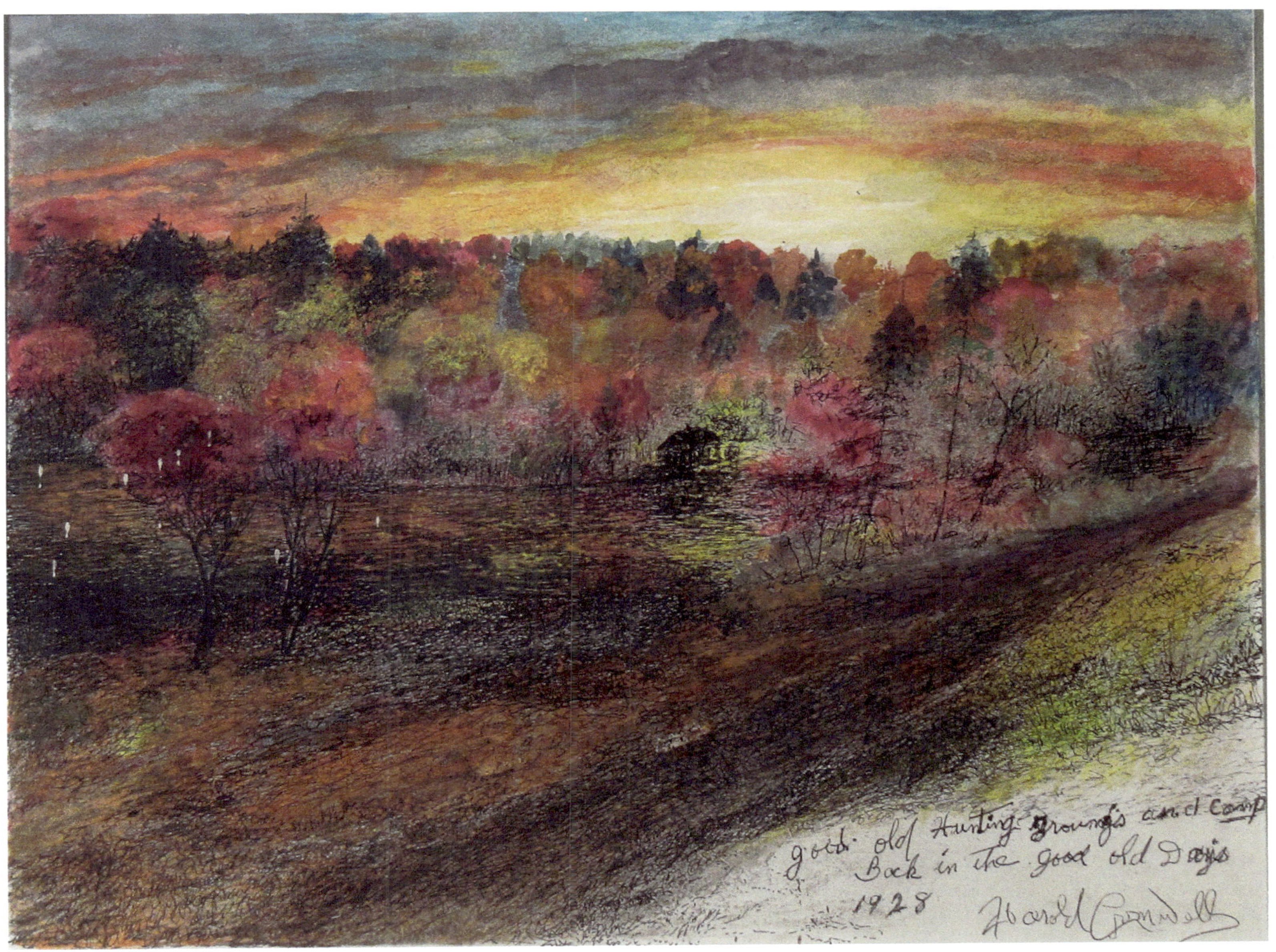

good old Hunting grounds and Camp
Back in the good old Days
1928
Harold Cromwell

Farming Back in the Good Old Days of 1920-1931

Pen and ink – 10 ½" x 12 ¾"

Bottom right:
Farming Back in old Day's of 1920-1931

Back:

C2009.0029
Estate # 16
Title: Farming Back in old Days of 1920-31
Signature: Harold Cromwell

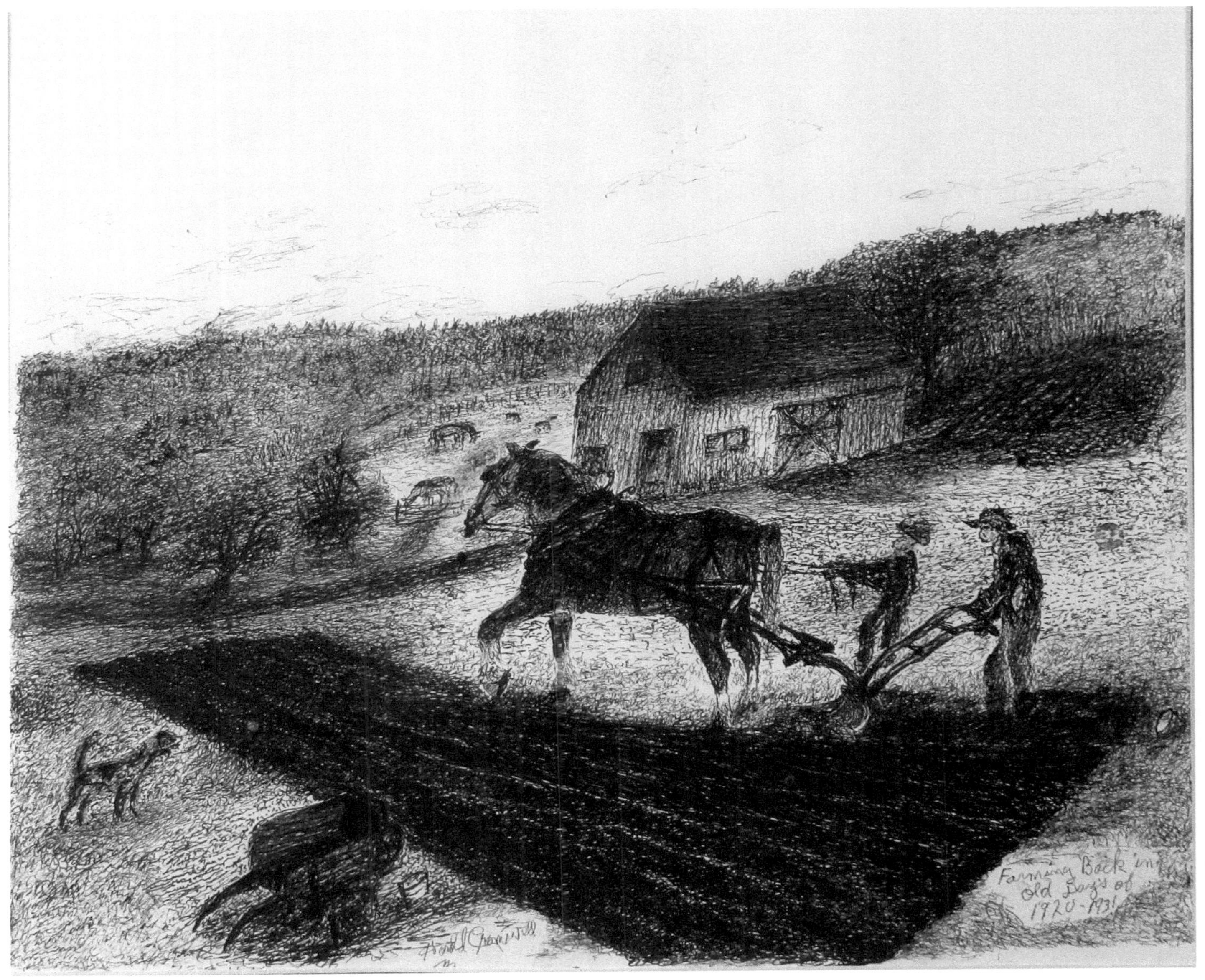
Farming Back in
Old Days of
1920-1931
Harold Cromwell

Cats Will Keep the Birds out of Your Garden

Pen and ink – 12 ¾" x 19"

Back:

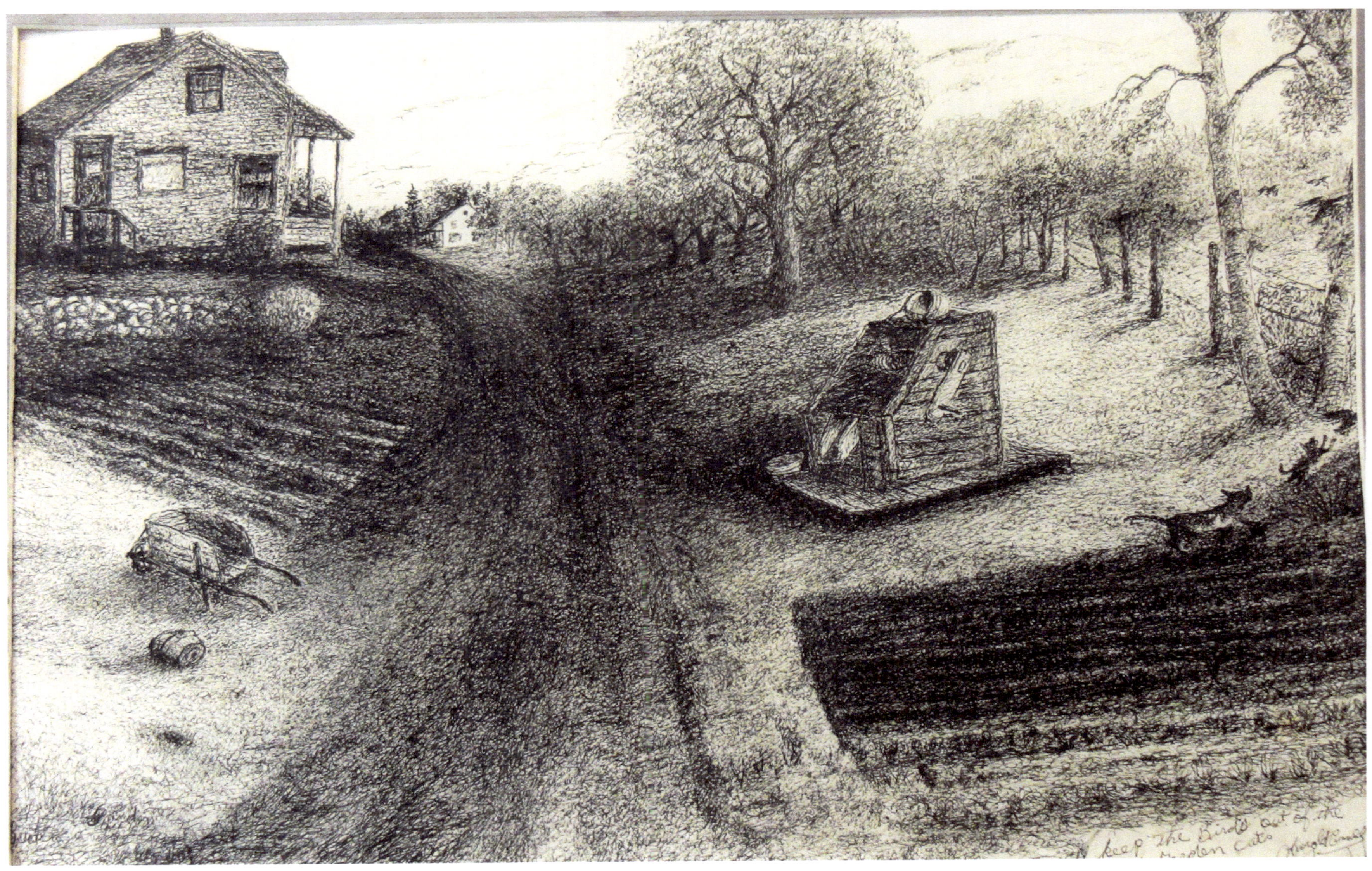

Back in the Good Old Days

Pen and ink – 7" x 15"

Back:

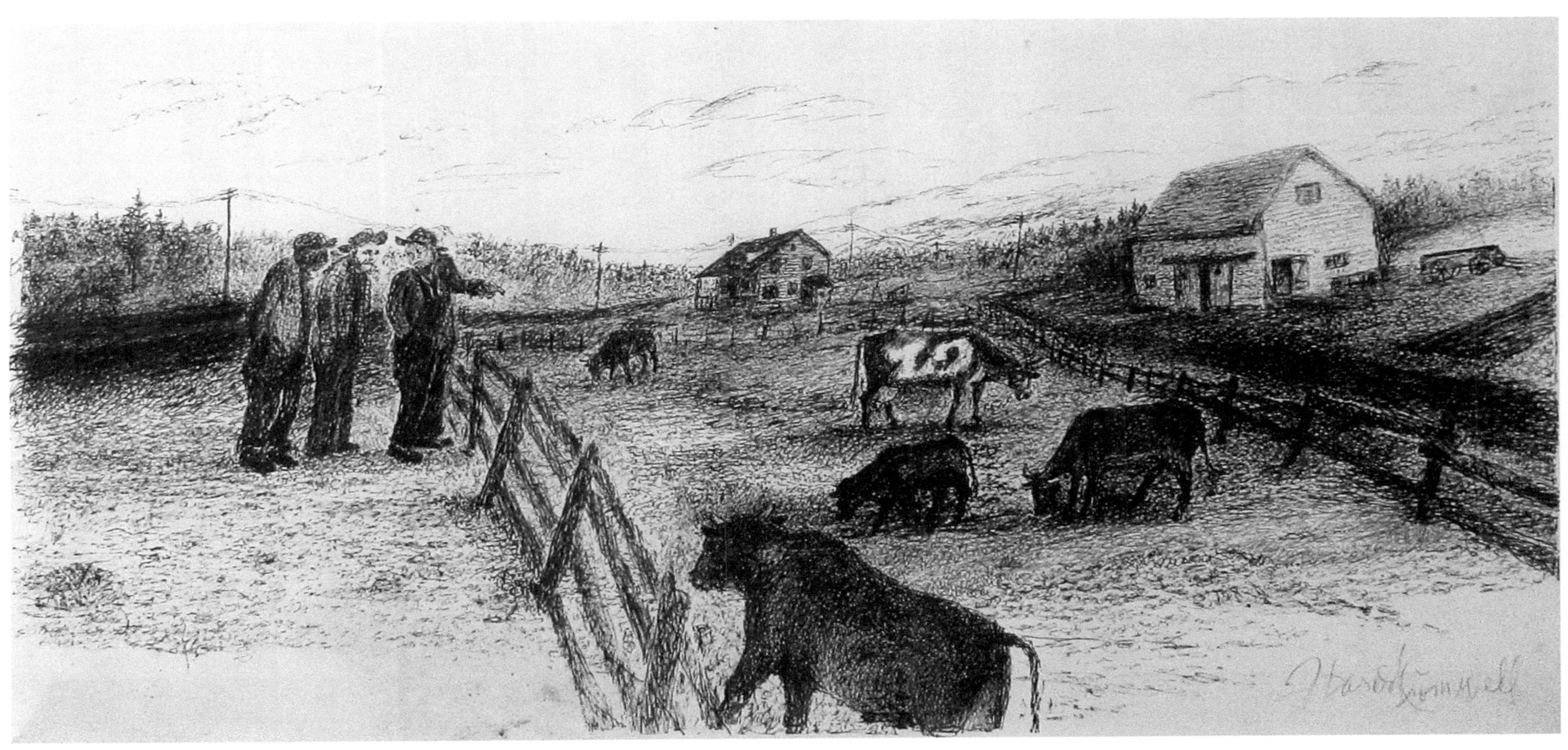

The Old Has Ben 1932 Fishing Walf

11 1/4" diameter wooden disk, pen and ink

Top:
The Old Has Ben 1932 Fishishing Walf

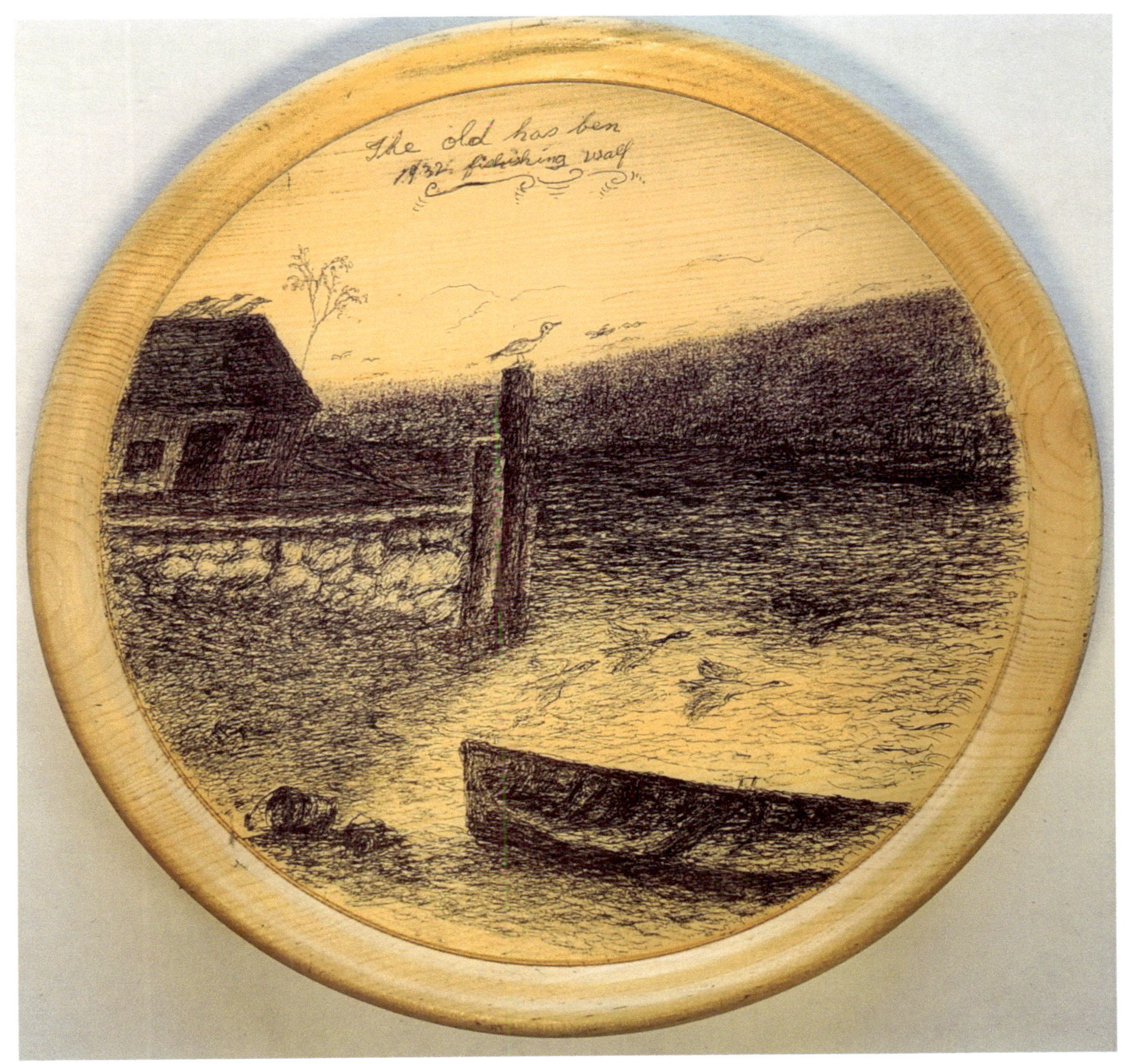
The old has ben
1932 fishing warf

Soup and Coffee 10 Cents Each

10" diameter paper plate (Chinet); pen and ink

Top:
Lunch an Bar
Beer 10¢
Coffe 10¢

Bottom:
Soup an Coffe
¢10- 10 each
Halifax
Back in 1935

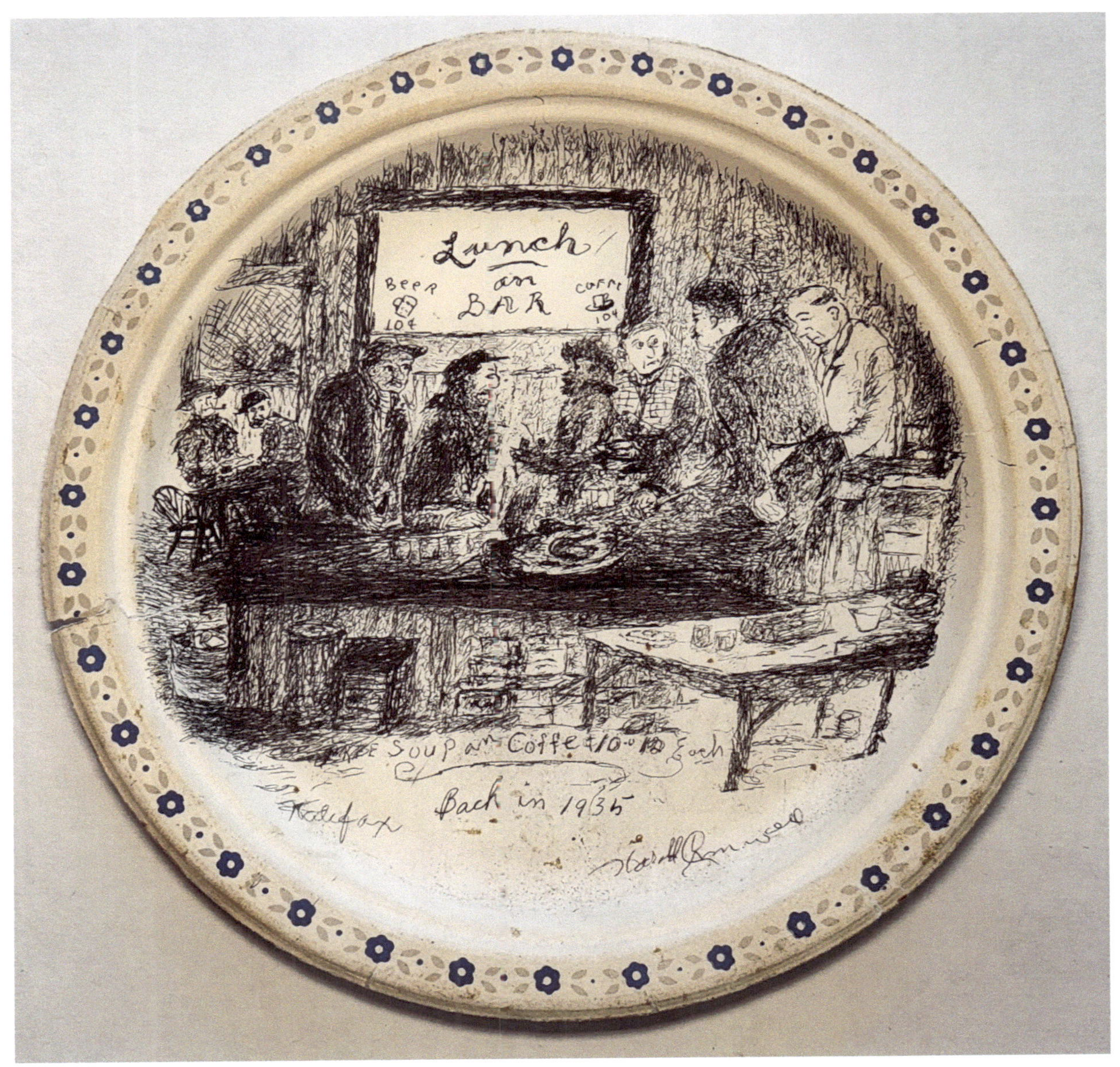

Lunch
an
BAR
BEER
10¢
COFFE
10¢
SOUP an Coffe 10..10 Each
Back in 1935
Halifax
Harold Cromwell

Clam Digers

11 1/4" diameter wooden disk; pen and ink

Bottom:
Clam Digers

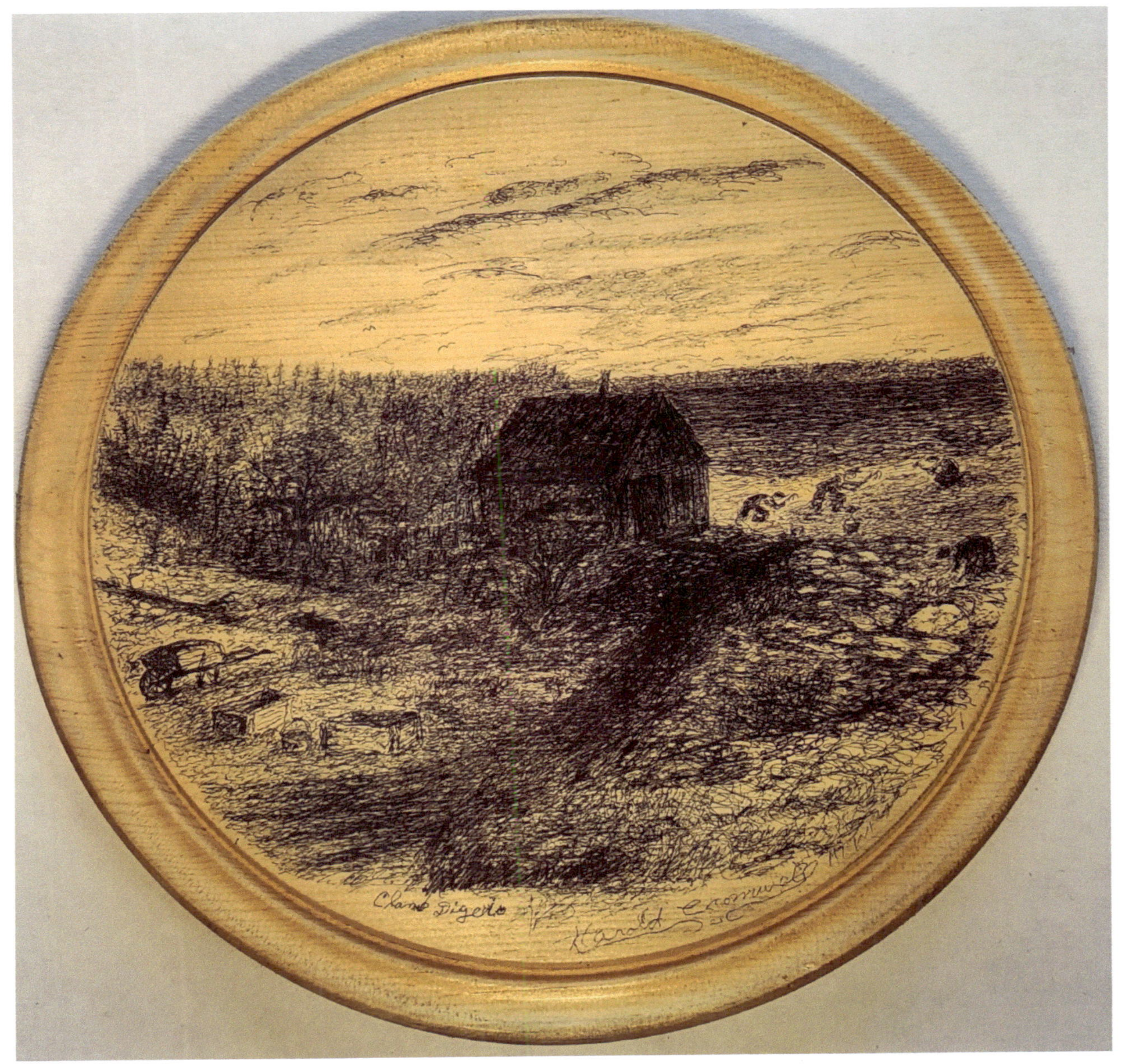

Acknowledgements

Harold Cromwell was a prominent figure in the cultural life of the Annapolis Region for many years. In 2021, The Annapolis Region Community Arts Council (ARCAC) decided it would be of great value to the community to organize an exhibition of Cromwell's artworks at ARTSPLACE entitled "Back in the Old Days: The Art of Harold Cromwell", September 9-October 28, 2023. The art being shown was selected from the Cromwell family's personal collection. ARCAC is especially grateful to his daughters, Natasha Cromwell and Clara Cromwell, and his grandsons, Karlon DeZylva-Adhihetty and Phillip Bailey, for their enthusiastic support of the project.

ARCAC would also like to acknowledge the participation of Ray Cronin, essayist for this publication and contributor to the "Community Conversation" about Cromwell's life and art that took place on September 9, 2023. Special thanks to Moose House Publications for its commitment to this project. Credit also goes to Wendy Salsman for her photographs of Cromwell's work and Phil Secord for his professional framing and matting of some of the artworks. Sissiboo Landing, Weymouth's Cultural and Interpretive Centre, also provided background information on Harold Cromwell's life.

ARCAC staff Sophie Paskins, Gallery Director, and Geoff Agombar, Assistant Gallery Director, deserve recognition for their professional involvement in the project. Volunteers Ted Lind and Terry Drahos willingly committed their time to insure that this project moved forward.

Special thanks to the Municipality of the County of Annapolis and Arts Nova Scotia for their financial support of "Back in the Old Days: Art by Harold Cromwell".

And thank you to Moose House Publications for its commitment to this project, and to artist Geoff Butler for suggesting we work with them.

About ARTSPLACE

ARTSPLACE is a contemporary gallery and arts centre in Annapolis Royal, Nova Scotia, operated by the Annapolis Region Community Arts Council (ARCAC).

ARCAC was founded in 1982 by a group of artists who wanted to share their work and ideas with each other and their community. ARCAC is a registered charitable organization. In 1996, ARCAC acquired its own building, known as ARTSPLACE. In 1998, ARTSPLACE was awarded Canada Council funding to present contemporary, visual arts as an artist-run centre.

ARTSPLACE has four galleries, residency and pop-up studio/gallery and space for workshops and performances. ARTSPLACE's juried, professional visual arts exhibitions are programmed by an arm's-length committee of the Board, comprised 100% of artists. ARCAC is funded by the Canada Council for the Arts (CCA) and the NS Dept. of Communities, Culture and Heritage (CCH), and through memberships, donations and fundraising contributions.

ARCAC has developed a province-wide and national reputation for generating interesting activities and opportunities within the community. Membership is composed of approximately 200 individuals and families who believe that involvement in the arts makes life both rewarding and fun. ARCAC runs a year-round schedule of workshops, classes, readings, screenings, talks and special events. Through a Scholarship Fund, ARCAC assists students of all ages who wish to pursue art-related courses of study.

ARTSPLACE's vision is to share stimulating work and strengthen artistic life in the Annapolis Region. Creating environments for art and arts practitioners to thrive is key to ARCAC's work, as is supporting audiences in their growth, awareness, and excitement about art.

Back in the Old Days

About Ray Cronin

Ray Cronin is a Nova Scotia-based writer, curator, and editor, living in Mi'kma'ki and the district of Sipekne'katik, the ancestral and un-ceded territory of the Mi'kmaq people. He is the author of fourteen books on Canadian art, including *Alan Syliboy: Culture is Our Medicine* (Gaspereau Press), *Alex Colville: Life & Work* (Arts Canada Institute), *Our Maud: The Life, Art and Legacy of Maud Lewis* (Art Gallery of Nova Scotia), *Gerald Ferguson: Thinking of Painting* (Gaspereau Press), *John Greer: Hard Thought* (Gaspereau Press), *Mary Pratt: Life & Work* (Arts Canada Institute), and *Colleen Wolstenholme: Complications* (Gaspereau Press).

Cronin is the author of numerous catalogue essays for Canadian art galleries, as well as articles for Canadian and American art magazines. In 2012 he received the Christina Sabat Award for Critical Review in the Arts. He was the Visual Arts Columnist for the *Daily Gleaner* (Fredericton, NB) and *Here* (St. John, NB) and is the Editor-in-Chief of *Billie: Visual Art Atlantic*.

He worked at the Art Gallery of Nova Scotia as Curator (2001-2007) and as Director and CEO (2007-2015). He is the founding curator of the Sober Art Award.

He is a graduate of the Nova Scotia College of Art and Design (Bachelor of Fine Arts) and the University of Windsor (Master of Fine Arts).